MY BOOK OF
Bible Stories

© MCMLXII, The Standard Publishing Company

a FRANCES HOOK picture book
with stories by WANDA HAYES

© MCMLXIV, The STANDARD PUBLISHING Company ● Cincinnati, Ohio ● Printed in U.S.A.

NOAH
Built a Boat

Many, many years ago God spoke to a good man named Noah. He said, "Noah, I want you and your three sons to build a big boat. This boat will be a house for you, your wife, and your sons and their wives."

Noah and his sons obeyed God. They built a big boat, just as God told them. When it was finished, God said, "Take two of every kind of animal and bird into the boat; take enough food for your family and for the animals." Noah did just what God said.

When Noah and his family and all the animals were inside the big boat, God closed the door. Soon Noah and his family heard, "Pitter patter, pitter patter." It was the sound of rain, and it grew louder and louder. It rained and it rained. It rained for forty days and forty nights. But Noah and his family and all the animals in the big boat were safe and dry.

After the rain stopped, the big boat stopped on top of a mountain. When the land was dry again, Noah and his family came out of the boat. All of the animals and birds came outside too. Noah prayed, "Thank you, God for taking care of us."

—From Genesis 6:13—8:22

JACOB and ESAU
Lived in a Tent

Isaac and Rebekah were very happy. God gave them two strong baby boys. They were twins. One was named Esau and the other one was named Jacob.

God told Rebekah, "Your sons will be the leaders of two big groups of people someday."

Rebekah took good care of the sons God had given to her and Isaac. She taught them to love and obey God.

Jacob was a very quiet boy, who liked to stay near his tent-house and take care of sheep.

Esau liked to go into the fields and hunt animals for food, as his father did.

Rebekah watched Jacob and Esau grow. She was very pleased with her two sons. Isaac was very pleased with his two sons.

And when Jacob and Esau grew up and became men, each of them was the leader of a big group of people, just as God had promised.

—From Genesis 25:19-27

MOSES
Slept in a Basket

Long ago a kind mother carried a little basket bed she had made for her baby boy. The mother and her daughter walked to the river with the baby in the basket bed.

"Shhh! Do not cry," the mother said to the sweet baby. "Go to sleep. God will take care of you." Then she set the basket bed on the water, among the tall grass. She was hiding her sweet little boy so the wicked king would not kill him. "Miriam, stay close and watch your baby brother," the mother said.

The baby's mother left, and Miriam watched the little basket bed very closely. Soon a princess came to the river. "What do I hear?" she said. "It sounds like a baby crying." The princess looked and saw the basket bed. She saw the sweet little baby boy. "I will not let the king hurt you," the princess said.

Miriam said, "I know a good nurse who will take care of the baby for you."

"Go and bring her," said the princess.

Do you know whom Miriam brought to take care of her brother? It was their very own mother. She must have thanked God very much for letting the princess find the baby.

The princess said, "I shall name the baby Moses."

And Moses grew to be a good helper for God.

—From Exodus 2:1-10; Hebrews 11:23

RUTH
Helped an Old Woman

"Good-by," said Naomi. "I must go back to the city where I used to live. You must go to your city, too, Ruth."

"No," said Ruth. "You are my dear friend, and I shall not leave you alone. I will go home with you. Your friends will be my friends. I will love and obey God as you do."

So Naomi and Ruth, two women who loved God, walked together to Bethlehem where Naomi used to live.

"Look, it is our old friend, Naomi," the women in Bethlehem said.

And Naomi probably said, "This is my friend, Ruth. She has come to live with me so I will not be lonely."

Ruth did something else for Naomi, too. When they needed food, Ruth went to a field where the men gathered tall, yellow grain. Sometimes they left a little grain on the ground. Ruth was allowed to have it. She gathered the grain in her apron and took it home to Naomi. Naomi made flour from the grain, and she made bread from the flour.

Ruth and Naomi said, "Thank you God, for taking care of us." And Naomi probably prayed, "Thank you God, for my dear friend, Ruth."

—From Ruth 1, 2

HANNAH
Gave Her Son to God

Hannah wanted a baby boy more than anything else in the world. So when Hannah and her husband went to God's house to worship, Hannah kneeled and prayed to God. She said, "God in heaven, please give me a boy baby. I shall take care of him and teach him to love you. He will work for you all his life."

Hannah and her husband went home. One day God gave Hannah a little boy baby, just as she had wanted. Hannah was very happy. She said, "I shall call the baby Samuel."

Hannah took good care of Samuel. She fed him and washed him and put clean clothes on him.

When Samuel was a little boy, his mother dressed him in his best clothes and took him to God's house. Hannah went to keep her promise to God. She said to Eli, the man who took care of God's house, "This is the boy God gave me. This is the boy I prayed for. Take care of him and teach him how to please God."

And Eli did take care of Samuel. Samuel lived in God's house and became a good helper for God.

—From 1 Samuel 1

SAMUEL
Heard God Call

Samuel liked living in God's house. He liked helping Eli. There was a lot of work to do, and Samuel was a good worker.

Samuel opened the big doors of God's house in the morning. Perhaps he helped sweep the floors and dust the furniture. Samuel probably did whatever Eli told him to do. There were many ways a boy like Samuel could help.

One night after Samuel had gone to bed, he heard a voice call, "Samuel."

Who could it be? Samuel sat up in bed. "It must be Eli," he thought. So Samuel called out, "Here I am." And he ran to Eli's bed and said, "I came because I heard you call me."

But Eli said, "I did not call you, Samuel. Go back to bed."

Again the voice called, "Samuel."

Samuel hurried to Eli, but Eli said, "I did not call you, my son. Go back to bed."

And the voice called Samuel again. But this time Eli told Samuel, "Go back to bed, and when you hear the voice again, say, 'Speak, Lord; for your servant hears you.' "

And that's what Samuel did because it was God's voice calling him. God had a special message to tell His good helper, Samuel.

—From 1 Samuel 3:1-10

DAVID
Sang About God

David was a shepherd boy. He took care of his father's sheep. He led the sheep and the little lambs to green fields where they ate all the green grass they wanted. And when the sheep were thirsty, David took them to a stream of water to get a drink.

Sometimes David made songs and sang them to his sheep while he played his harp. David sang many songs about God. When David thought about God, he felt just like a sheep; and God was the shepherd who took care of him. David wrote this song about God:

God is my shepherd; I do not need anything.
He leads me in green fields and by still waters.
He makes me strong.
He teaches me to do what is right.
I shall never be afraid of bad things because God
    is with me.
I am very happy.
God will be good and kind to me all my life,
And I shall live in the house of God forever.

—From Psalm 23

DAVID
Became a King

David took care of his father's sheep near the town of Bethlehem. David obeyed his father, and he obeyed his heavenly Father, God.

Because David was good, God took care of him. When a lion took one of David's sheep, David went after the lion and killed it. He brought the sheep safely back home to the other sheep. God helped David kill the lion. When a bear took one of David's sheep, God helped David kill the bear.

One time while David was watching his sheep, someone came running toward him calling, "David, David, come to your house. A man has come to visit your father, and he wants to see you."

When David came to the house, he met the man. He was Samuel, who had been a boy in God's house. Now Samuel was an old man. God had sent Samuel to find the next king for His people. And David, the shepherd boy, was the one God had chosen.

"When you are a man, you will be the king," Samuel told David.

God was pleased with David. David was a good shepherd boy, and God knew he would be a good king.

—From 1 Samuel 16:1-13; 17:34-37

A SERVANT GIRL
Helped Her Master

Naaman was the captain of an army of the king. He was a great man, but Naaman was very sick.

A young girl who helped take care of Naaman's wife said, "I wish that Naaman could visit God's helper, Elisha, in my country. He would make Naaman well."

When Naaman heard what the little girl said, he decided to go see Elisha and find out whether he could make him well. So Naaman rode to the land where Elisha lived.

When Elisha heard that Naaman was in his country, he sent someone to tell Naaman, "Go and wash seven times in the Jordan River, and you will be well."

But when Naaman heard this, he was angry. "I thought Elisha would come and make me well. I do not want to wash in the Jordan River."

Naaman's servant said, "Elisha did not tell you to do something hard. Do what he said."

So Naaman obeyed Elisha. He went to the Jordan River and washed—one time—two times—three times —four times—five times—six times—seven times. When Naaman came out of the water the seventh time, he was well. Naaman could hardly believe it. He was so happy he went back to Elisha and said, "I know that there is one God. God made me well."

Naaman was glad God made him well, and he was thankful for the little girl who helped him.

—From 2 Kings 5:1-15

ELISHA
Had Kind Friends

Elisha walked through many towns telling people how to obey God. Everyone who saw Elisha knew that he was a good man.

One day when Elisha came by a house, the woman who lived there said, "Hello, Elisha. Come and eat with my husband and me. We are glad to share our food with you. Come and rest in our house. You must be tired."

So Elisha ate with the man and woman. And every time Elisha walked through that town, he ate with them.

One day the woman said to her husband, "Elisha is one of God's helpers. Let's help him by building a little room for him. We can put a bed, a table, a chair, and a lamp in the room. Then Elisha will have a nice place to stay when he comes here again."

The next time Elisha visited the man and woman, they probably said, "Elisha, we have a surprise for you. We have built your own room with a bed, a table, a chair, and a lamp. We want you to use this room because you are God's helper."

And every time Elisha visited the man and woman, he stayed in his own nice room. And Elisha prayed, "Thank you, God, for these kind people and for this room."

—From 2 Kings 4:8-11

DANIEL
Prayed to God

Daniel prayed to God every morning, every afternoon, and every night. Daniel thanked God for many things.

In the country where Daniel lived only a few people prayed to God. Some of these people did not like Daniel. They asked the king to make a law saying that anyone who prayed to God would be put into a den of lions.

But Daniel was not afraid. Every day he prayed three times in front of the window. He thanked God just as he always did.

Then the king had to put Daniel in the lions' den. But the king was a friend of Daniel. He did not want Daniel to be hurt. The king was sorry he had made the law. He was sorry that his friend Daniel was in the den of lions.

After Daniel had been in the lions' den all night, the king hurried there and called, "Daniel, did your God take care of you?"

"Yes," said Daniel. "God sent an angel to shut the lions' mouths. They did not hurt me."

Then the king let Daniel go back to his house. And every day Daniel knelt in front of the window and prayed three times to God, just as he always did.

—From Daniel 6

JESUS
Made a Boy Well

One day a rich man, who worked for a king, came to Jesus and said, "My son is sick in another city. Please come and make him well. He is so sick that his mother and I are afraid he will die."

Jesus knew that the rich man believed He could make his son well. So Jesus told the man, "Go home. Your son is alive."

The rich man believed Jesus. He hurried back to his own city as fast as he could. And before he even got to his house, his servants came and said, "Your son is alive. He is all right."

The rich man knew Jesus had made his son well. And everyone in his house knew that Jesus had made the little boy well.

Now the little boy could run and play again. He could hug his father and mother. He could do everything he used to do. The rich man and his wife and little boy were very happy. They were very thankful for Jesus.

—From John 4:46-54

A BOY
Gave His Lunch to Jesus

Wherever Jesus went crowds of people followed Him. Some came to hear Him tell about God and about how they should live. Sick people came to Jesus so He would make them well.

One day a big crowd of people listened to Jesus nearly all day. Jesus taught the people, and He healed some of them. The people were so interested in Jesus they didn't even go home to eat. Jesus knew the people were hungry so He asked His helpers, "Where can we buy bread for these people?"

Philip said, "We do not have enough money to buy even one bite of bread for everyone."

Then Andrew said, "There is a boy here who has five loaves of bread and two fish. But they will not feed all of these people."

Jesus took the bread and fish the boy gave to Him. Then He told everyone to sit down on the soft grass. Jesus thanked God for the boy's lunch.

Then something very special happened. Jesus gave His helpers the bread and fish to give to the people. Instead of five loaves and two fish, there was more and more. There was enough for everyone. There were even twelve basketfuls of food left after everyone had eaten.

The people knew that only God could have made so much food from one boy's small lunch.

—From John 6:1-13

TIMOTHY
Taught About Jesus

Timothy was a good boy. He had a kind mother named Eunice and a kind grandmother named Lois. Timothy's mother and grandmother loved and obeyed God. They both taught Timothy to love and obey God.

Timothy loved to hear his grandmother read from God's Book. She probably read stories about Moses and Samuel and David and many other helpers of God. Perhaps Timothy thought, "Maybe someday I can be a helper for God. Maybe I can be as brave as the men God's Book tells about."

Timothy grew older. He learned more and more about God's Book. He learned to read and study it by himself. One day a man named Paul came to the town where Timothy and Eunice and Lois lived. He taught Timothy and his mother and grandmother about Jesus, God's Son. Paul said, "Timothy, you can tell others about Jesus, too. Come and help me teach people in other countries how to obey God."

Timothy probably was very excited. "Paul wants me to go with him," thought Timothy. So Timothy and Paul traveled to many different cities and countries. Sometimes they walked, and sometimes they sailed on a ship. Timothy and Paul taught many people about Jesus. Timothy was a good, brave helper for Paul and for God.

—From Acts 16:1-5; 2 Timothy 1:3-5

DORCAS
Helped Many People

"Look at the dress Dorcas made for me!" said a happy little girl. "I love kind Dorcas. She made my pretty new dress."

Dorcas was a very good woman. She used her hands to help people in a special way. Dorcas made clothes for women who did not have very much money. And she made coats and dresses for poor children, too. Dorcas had many friends because she was so kind.

But one day Dorcas' friends were very sad. Dorcas was very, very sick. Soon Dorcas died. Her friends looked at the pretty coats and dresses Dorcas had made them. The people cried. "We will miss our good friend very much," they said.

But something happened. Two men brought Peter, one of Jesus helpers, to Dorcas' house. Peter went to the room where Dorcas was in bed. He knelt down and prayed to God. Then Peter said to Dorcas, "Get up."

And she did. Dorcas was alive again! Peter took Dorcas to her friends. Oh, how happy they were! They told everyone they saw, "God made Dorcas alive again. Our friend Dorcas is alive."

—From Acts 9:36-42

Do You Remember?

Try to remember the names if you can.
Then have someone read you the stories again.

Who lived in a boat with animals in it?
Who made a boy well again in a minute?

Name the twin boys who lived in a tent.
Who taught about Jesus wherever he went?

What baby slept in a basket bed?
Whom did Peter pray for when she was dead?

Who gathered grain for her friend every day?
Who kneeled by his window three times to pray?

Who prayed for a son—her only wish?
Who fed a crowd with five loaves and two fish?

What boy answered God when He called him one night?
Who made a man wash to make him all right?

What boy sang to God while he cared for his sheep?
Who gave Elisha a good place to sleep?

Every kind person in God's Book is true,
And each one of us can be God's helper, too.